crap
taxidermy

To my tiger mom, Wendy Su

See? I told you I'd publish a book one day.
Wait, this isn't what you had in mind? Fuck.

crap taxidermy

Kat Su

CASSELL ILLUSTRATED

An Hachette UK Company
www.hachette.co.uk

First published in Great Britain in 2014 by
Cassell, a division of Octopus Publishing Group Ltd
Endeavour House, 189 Shaftesbury Avenue
London WC2H 8JY
www.octopusbooks.co.uk

ISBN 978 1 84403 803 9

A CIP catalogue record for this book is available from the British Library.
Printed and bound in China.
10 9 8 7 6 5 4 3 2 1

Commissioning editor Hannah Knowles
Editor Pauline Bache
Art director Yasia Williams-Leedham
Designer and illustrator Abigail Read
Production controller Sarah-Jayne Johnson

contents

Introduction

Taxidermy is a multidisciplinary artform. A competent taxidermist has an encyclopedic knowledge of anatomy, the laser-like precision of a world-class surgeon and an artistic sensitivity to the physical world that rivals God Himself. The chances of a mere mortal mastering any of these traits is very slim, and the likelihood of becoming proficient in all three is virtually non-existent.

In the summer of 2009, I moved into an apartment in Brooklyn, New York, and aspired to give my sad living situation a touch of class by incorporating some dead animals into the decor. After scouring eBay and Etsy for taxidermy (a deer head to be precise), I quickly realized that the taxidermy available on the Internet could be classified into four categories:

1) Good taxidermy.
2) Bad taxidermy.
3) Weird-as-hell good taxidermy.
4) Weird-as-hell bad taxidermy.

Consequently, I launched the *Crappy Taxidermy* Tumblr to document the latter three categories. Since the site's creation, I have obsessively kept track of every bug-eyed, misshapen, awkward, or just-plain-wrong piece of taxidermy that I was able to find online. As the site grew, readers started submitting photographs of their own taxidermy, and sightings of crappy taxidermy that they had found in museums, roadside attractions, stores, art galleries or people's homes.

Considering all the weird, creepy taxidermy pictures I have accumulated on my hard drive since working on the *Crappy Taxidermy* blog, I had always speculated that I would be in jail by now for crimes against good taste.

However, I'm thrilled that the exact opposite has happened. This book is a celebration of crappy taxidermy and the eccentric and amazing people who create it. Regular taxidermy endeavours to give the illusion of life to the non-living, but crappy taxidermy highlights the subject's state of death due to the animal being contextualized in a completely surreal or absurd way. This book will present examples of taxidermy that is in a permanent state of rigor mortis, taxidermy that is so anatomically incorrect that it could be considered a crime against nature, and my personal favourite, taxidermy with hilarious over-the-top facial expressions.

The spirit of the book isn't meant to be disparaging, and I hope that people will delight in looking at the strange and preposterous specimens on display in these pages. A very special thank you to the taxidermists, fine artists, readers and well-travelled photographers who contributed the pictures in this book.

it's in the eyes

10 Fox with eye transplant
Spotted in Cairo, Egypt

Karate-loving lioness
Spotted in Yorkshire, United Kingdom

12 **Best friends forever**
Spotted in New York, USA

Earnest fox
Spotted in St Petersburg, Russia

13

14   **Fearsome barn owl**
Spotted in Ohiya, Sri Lanka

Flat wolf
Spotted in Rhodes, Greece

16 Extinct brown bear
Spotted in Newtown, Australia

Predatory brown bear
Spotted in Steyl, The Netherlands

18 Crusty panda
Spotted in Chengdu, China

Alien-eyed serval
Spotted in Kuching, Malaysia

20 Hungover cat
Spotted in Pyongsong, North Korea

Earless snow leopard
Spotted in Pokhara, Nepal

22 **Hungry hypnotized ocelot**
Spotted in Quetzaltenango, Guatemala

Attentive serval
Spotted in Stavanger, Norway

Cock-eyed Bornean cat
Spotted in Kuching, Malaysia

dynamic poses

26 **Incongruous rabbit**
Spotted in Jubail, Saudi Arabia

Secret life of opossums
Spotted in Napier, New Zealand

Pouncing Asian leopard-cat
Spotted in Kuching, Malaysia

30 **Rigid bobcat**
Spotted in North Carolina, USA

Scared, Inquisitive and Bored
Spotted in Pyongsong, North Korea

Riding the wolf bus
Spotted in Gansu Province, China

34 Fully alert bobcat
Spotted in New York, USA

grin & bear it

على رجلين ومنهم من يمشي على أربع يخلق الله ما يشاء إن الله

Groaning bovine
Spotted in London, United Kingdom

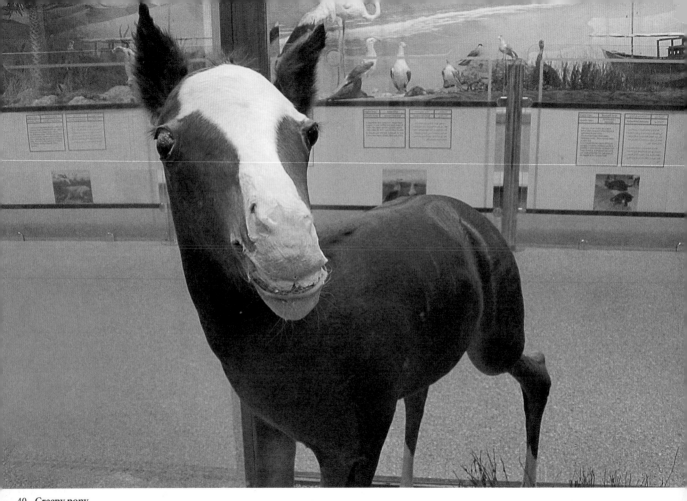

40 **Creepy pony**
Spotted in Jubail, Saudi Arabia

Tabby gymnastics
Spotted in Moscow, Russia

41

42 Forty-a-day lion
Spotted in Qalqilya, State of Palestine

Leering hyena
Spotted in Jubail, Saudi Arabia

44 Tonsils the Lynx
Spotted in Oregon, USA

46 **Over-friendly dog**
Spotted in Gwangju, South Korea

Moth-eaten wolves
Spotted in Kochkor, Kyrgyzstan

improving on nature

50   Victorian ceiling fan
     Spotted in London, United Kingdom

Guinea pig knuckleduster
Spotted in Budapest, Hungary

Cyclops monster
Spotted in Jubail, Saudi Arabia

21.10.14.3-10

54 **Furious wolpertinger**
Spotted in New York, USA

Curious wolpertinger
Spotted in Rothenburg, Germany

Siamese sheep
Spotted in London, United Kingdom

58 Ratipede (scientific name *Rattus brachipodia*)
Spotted in Georgia, USA

Creative beer bottles
Spotted in Brewdog advertisement

59

strange anatomy

Googly-eyed puffer fish
Spotted in Ulan Bator, Mongolia

64 Dieting fox
Spotted in Budapest, Hungary

Uncomfortable coyote
Spotted in Lake Titicaca, Peru

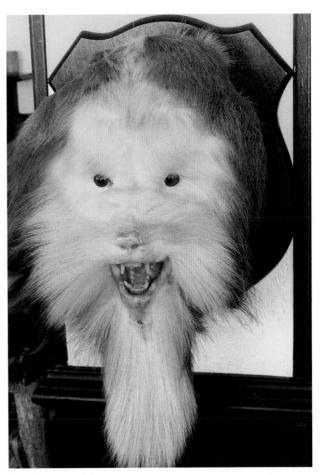

Tasteful 'Assquatch'
Spotted in London, United Kingdom

66 Fox-cat dual
Spotted in Qalqilya, State of Palestine

ЭМПЕРОР ОЦОН ШУВУУ

Aptenodytes forsteri

Emperor penguin

Crestfallen cat
Spotted in Pyongsong, North Korea

Fiesty jaguar
Spotted in Cuiaba, Brazil

Gangly rabbit
Spotted in Helsinki, Finland

70 Serene cows
Spotted in Budapest, Hungary

anthropomorphic

Irate mole
Spotted in New York, USA

78 Mid-death crisis
Spotted in Yorkshire, United Kingdom

Menacing rabbit
Spotted in Rhodes, Greece

Supermouse
Spotted in Paris, France

79

80 **Curtain-twitching opossum**
Spotted in Napier, New Zealand

Bushbaby
Spotted in Tauranga, New Zealand

82 Cowboy opossum
Spotted in Georgia, USA

Relaxed toad
Spotted in Sydney, Australia

get stuffed

How to Stuff your own Mouse

An interesting social consequence of working on a taxidermy blog is that everyone will start to ask you if you're a taxidermist. People are generally disappointed to find out that I'm actually a fashion designer, and that I was the kid who skipped Biology the day the class had to dissect a frog. Due to my squeamishness, I didn't think that I would ever see the day where I would have to do taxidermy but I needed to gain personal experience to execute this section of the book.

While I am by no means qualified to teach people how to stuff a mouse, an asset of working on a taxidermy blog is that I've met some bad ass and talented individuals who are also taxidermists. One of these people is Daisy Tainton. I first met Daisy at a taxidermy contest in Brooklyn in 2009, and I was immediately drawn to her bright pink hair and dry sense of humour. Daisy was on stage presenting dioramas of rhinoceros beetles in charming domestic settings (i.e. beetle sitting in a rocking chair knitting a sweater, beetle eating a plate of pasta alone), explaining that she was an Insect Preparator for the American Museum of Natural History, and that making

'Should I add boobs to him now? I suppose I can sort that out later.'
- Daisy

beetle dioramas was one of her hobbies. When a judge facetiously asked her if her beetles ever got rowdy, she retorted: 'No. They're quite sedate.' In addition to being good with bugs, Daisy has stuffed various small and medium sized mammals, birds, as well as various fantasy creatures courtesy of her healthy but perverse imagination. Another fun fact about Daisy is that she currently has a cat and a kitten in her freezer, despite being a vegetarian.

When I first approached Daisy to help me with this section of the book, I asked her to think of it as an 'idiot-proof guide to mouse taxidermy' in hopes that even the most clumsy and squeamish person (such as myself) could

Reader beware: whatever you do, DO NOT rupture the poop sack.

do an adequate job on this project. There isn't much you can do about squeamishness, but the final result is a guide to mouse taxidermy utilizing materials that are cheap, forgiving and easy to source. If you've ever been curious about taxidermy, I recommend grabbing a couple of funny sarcastic friends and using this tutorial as basis for a bizarre weekend adventure.

Total time: Approximately 2 hours

Preparation

Source your materials (see *right*). The most important one is your mouse, which can be procured from a pet store. I opted for frozen feeder mice (killed humanely by carbon dioxide gas) rather than a live one, for obvious reasons. The night before your taxidermy, remove the mouse from the freezer and allow to thaw in the refrigerator overnight. Be sure to liberate the mouse from its packaging if it is still wrapped. For storage, Daisy recommends using old plastic storage containers and resting the mouse on a bed of paper towels inside the container.

Daisy prefers working on a tray of loose borax as the borax will catch errant splashes of icky stuff that might occur during the process. Borax is a naturally occurring mineral compound that is available in the USA but is classed as toxic under EU regulations so borax substitutes are available in Europe and elsewhere. Because borax has chemical properties that make it a desiccant, preservative, fungicide and an insecticide, it has been commonly used in taxidermy as a moth-proofing and curing agent ever since substances like arsenic were phased out of use.

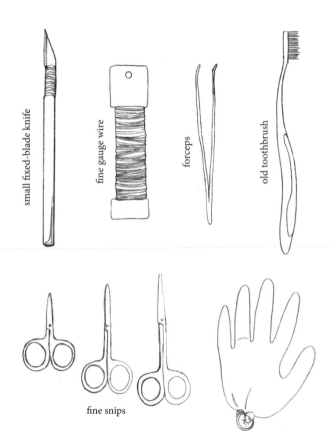

small fixed-blade knife

fine gauge wire

forceps

old toothbrush

fine snips

latex gloves (optional)

frozen mouse

pipe cleaners

children's self-drying clay

borax substitute

googly eyes or
ballpoint pins

aromatherapy
candle (optional)

wire cutters

thread

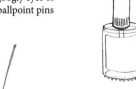

sewing needles   clear nail polish

Removal of the hide

1. Spread some borax substitute on the work surface. Lay the mouse on its back and make a straight cut down its underbelly with your knife. Be aware of the mouse's internal organs and try not to puncture through the abdominal walls. Daisy states that while this doesn't ruin the hide, 'the mess that it makes might ruin your day'. Once the incision is made, stretch the skin away from the muscles and use your knife or a pair of snips to help sever connective tissues (*a*).

2. Your goal is to create a 'mouse purse', where the hide is detached from the torso, but still attached at the limbs, head and tail. Because the leg bones are tiny and mostly covered in cartilage, it is acceptable to leave them intact and attached to the hide. To achieve this, peel back the skin from the legs until you get to the ankle (*b*). Once you reach this point, take your wirecutters or scissors and snip at the ankle joint to liberate the legs from the rest of the body.

3. Next, separate the inside of the head from the inside of the rest of the body. Take your wire cutters and snip at the neck; if you're wondering what happens to the brains and the eyes after you do this, the answer is that you will have to scoop them out later.

5. To scoop out the brains, insert your knife into the skull cavity and remove the wet tissue. You probably won't be able to get everything, so make sure you pack a lot of borax substitute into the head after you finish this step. Repeat the scooping part of this step with the eyes (*d*).

6. To cure the mouse hide, rub and clean the hide in the borax substitute.

4. At this point, the hide of your mouse should only be attached at the tail and the tail will need to be de-gloved. While this step is optional, Daisy highly recommends trying this step as it will allow you to manipulate the tail later. Otherwise, the tail will get withered and brittle as it dries. With de-gloving, the trick is to find a balance between firm and gentle, as the tail can tear very easily. Roll back the hide until you get a clear view of the base of the tail and use your fingers to push against the fold at the skin to extricate the skin from the bone structure (*c*). If you accidentally flip the tail inside out, use a pair of forceps or tweezers to rectify the situation.

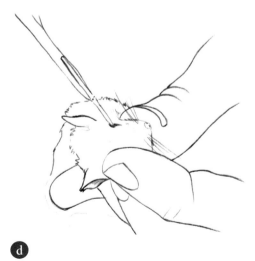

Stuffing the mouse

7. Get your mouse properly wired. Cut off a piece of a pipe cleaner and gently insert it through the tail. Next, cut off four pieces of fine gauge wire and carefully string it through the mouse's limbs until it pierces through to the outside (*e*). There's no need to be exact here, as you can always snip excess later and the wire will allow you to manipulate the position of its arms and legs.

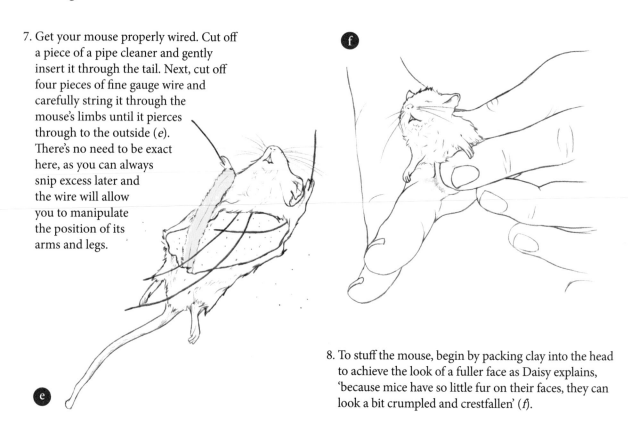

8. To stuff the mouse, begin by packing clay into the head to achieve the look of a fuller face as Daisy explains, 'because mice have so little fur on their faces, they can look a bit crumpled and crestfallen' (*f*).

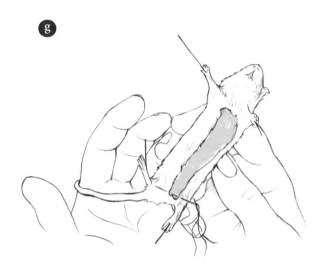

g

incision closed with the needle and thread and keep the seam allowance small (*g*). At this point, the clay and the wires will still be malleable. Position your mouse however you want; a sitting position is probably easiest though (*h*).

h

9. Next, make a small pancake with the clay and then line the interior of the pelt. Use your judgement to determine the amount of clay that you should use, bearing in mind that there is typically 10 per cent shrinkage after the clay fully dries. Stitch the

The finishing touches

10. To set in the eyes, cut the ballpoint pins into 6mm (¼in) nubs and pierce the pins through the eye sockets (*i*). You can also use another pin to manipulate the skin around the eye to create lids. Daisy also likes to run some nailpolish over the eyeball to give the mouse an extra hint of life. If you're not using pins and want to make crappy taxidermy, use an adhesive to glue some googly eyes over the eye.

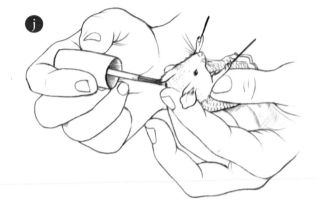

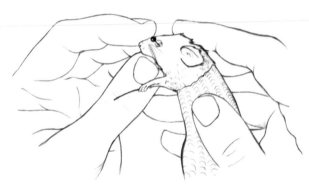

11. Next, take the clear nail polish and run it over the ears (*j*). This will give the ears more structure and stop them from folding in on themselves; it also instantly makes your mouse look perkier and more life-like. Keep an eye on the ears as they dry because their natural proclivity is to collapse. Finally, take an old toothbrush and gently groom the mouse; toothbrush, borax substitute and some scrubbing will work out any blood stains still in the fur. Set your mouse to dry, and when it is dry, snip off the extra wire.

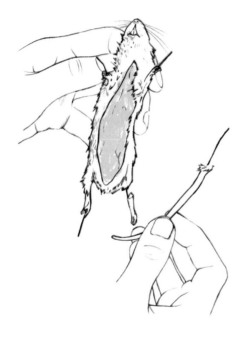

When accidents happen

Don't feel bad if accidents happen along the way. As an accident-prone person, I amputated two tails and one hind leg while I was stuffing my three mice. Daisy says that when this happens, you just have to improvise: 'If you're making a diorama, and your mouse unexpectedly loses a leg, you'll know where you should probably put the miniature table.' Since I wasn't working with any furniture props, I salvaged my amputated parts by stringing wire through them and reattaching the pieces to the main body with hot glue. Clearly, it's less than ideal, but it was still a workable solution for my purposes.

Mark Goldberg, Ken Krzeminski, Daisy Tainton, Meredith Zanotta, Daniel Pianetti, Jonas Diamant, Dana Melniz, Kayleigh Wanzer, Patricia Chang, Sarah Goldberg, Karin Reichert-Frei, Lisa Wolpert, Lawrence Swint, Yunusa Kenchi, Adam Cornish, Mark Goldblatt, Henry Welt, Allison Hunter, Tiffany Beveridge, Hannah Knowles, Pauline Bache, Tumblr & Octopus Books!

Finally, this book would not have been possible without these contributors:
Alexander Bunk (www.alexanderbunke.de), taxidermy by Cas Groooters (www.casperscreatures.com) 53; Alison Oddy (Flickr: WorldOfOddy) 11; Andrea (Flickr: hownowbrowncow2) 35; Andreas Vermulean 47; Andrew Lancaster, taxidermy by Andrew Lancaster 56, 81; Andrew Murray (Flickr: MrAndrewMurray) 10; Andy Deemer (www.asiaobscura.com) 63; Aodhnait Donnelly 79l; Becky King (Flickr: Mandy_Moon), taxidermy by Becky King 58; bighunter252 (eBay: bighunter252) 30; Bjørn Christian Tørrissen, (www.bjornfree.com) 14r, 20, 32, 45, 68l, 68r; Brad Traynor, taxidermy by Brad Traynor 82r; BrewDog UK (www.brewdog.com) 59; Brian Glucroft (www.isidorsfugue.com) 18; Chris Fraser 46; Christian Novak 55; Daniel Tepper 31, 38, 42, 66; David Haberthür (Flickr: habi) 14l; Emily Binard (Etsy: ebinard), The Gowanus Mermouse 76r, Road Kill's Revenge 77; Emma Quail 33; Géza Szöllősi (www.szollosi.eu), photography by Krisztián Zana (krisztianzana.com), Successful Hunting! 2007 28r, Boxer 2007 51l, Fox No.2 2010 64, Cows 2013 70; Hannah Knowles, taxidermy from The Viktor Wynd Museum of Curiosities 39, 50, 57; Hannah Knowles 65r; Ivie Morgan, taxidermy by Ivie Morgan 41; James Castleden (www.jamescastleden.com) 26, 40, 43, 51r; Jessie Hanz (Flickr: jessiebluejay) 71; Jon Chew (Flickr: Jonny_Chew) 19, 23, 29; Jon McClintock (Flickr: JonMcclintock) 21; Judit Aus 15; Julie Dermansky (www.jsdart.com) 28l; Karin 17; Kate Perris (Flickr: Dansette) 80; Kat Su 12, 34, 54, 75; Kenneth Gjesdal (Flickr: Gjesdal) 22r; Marco Repola (Flickr: istolethetv) 67, 74; Megan Manley (Flickr: TornadoGrrrl) 22l; Misha Davids (Flickr: Misha1138) 13; Mrrranda Tarrow 44; Paul Lim (Flickr: Fudj) 27, 76l; Sam Friedman (Flickr: Friedpixphoto) 79r; Sam Judson (Flickr: SamJudson) 65l; Sarah Burhouse, taxidermy by Sarah Burhouse (Etsy: snailsales) 78, 83; Sirja Ellen (Flickr: shaluna) 69; Thomas Monin (www.thomasmonin.com), Mafias I 2008, courtesy of Galerie Barnoud, Dijon, photograph by Phillippe Blanc 52; Tim Bradshaw 16; T.J. Edmond 82l; Yang Maoyuan, Horse No.3 2003, photograph by Yang Maoyuan 62.
Get Stuffed: Taxidermy by Daisy Tainton, source photographs by Meredith Zanotta.

The Usborne
Little Book of the
Seashore

First published in 2006 by Usborne Publishing Ltd.,
Usborne House, 83-85 Saffron Hill, London EC1N 8RT, England.
www.usborne.com

Printed in Dubai

The Usborne
Little Book of the
Seashore

Laura Howell

Designed by Michael Hill,
Laura Hammonds and Kate Rimmer

Digital illustration by Keith Furnival

Consultants: Dr Margaret Rostron
and Dr Roger Trend

Edited by Kirsteen Rogers

Internet links

There are lots of fun websites where you can find out more about the seashore. We have created links to some of the best sites on the Usborne Quicklinks Website. To visit the sites, go to www.usborne-quicklinks.com and type the keywords "little seashore". Here are some of the things you can do on the Internet:

❀ Explore a virtual rock pool
❀ Pick up lots of tips on building spectacular sand sculptures
❀ Find out about seashore conservation and how to get involved

Seashore pictures to download

Pictures marked with a ✳ in this book can be downloaded from the Usborne Quicklinks Website. These pictures are for personal use only and must not be used for commercial purposes.

Internet safety

The websites recommended in Usborne Quicklinks are regularly reviewed. However, the content of a website may change at any time and Usborne Publishing is not responsible for the content of websites other than its own. We recommend that children are supervised while on the Internet.

Contents

Beside the seaside

Shores and coasts are where the sea meets the land. From craggy cliffs to golden beaches, they are excellent places to explore and hunt for unique wildlife.

Homes for all

Wind, salt spray and lack of shelter can make life by the sea challenging, but many plants and animals are suited to it. Every coastal landscape, from mud to rocks, offers some living thing the conditions it needs for survival.

Gulls are one of the few animals that can be found on all types of shores.

Sandy shores

People usually visit sandy beaches to relax in the sun. Sunlight is less appealing to many shore animals, though, as too much of it dries out their fragile bodies. The creatures that live here are mostly hidden away under the sand, or beneath rocks.

Although this beach looks empty of life, hundreds of worms and shelled animals could be buried in the sand.

Rocky shores

Despite being one of the harshest seashore environments, rocky coasts are home to a marvellous mixture of animals and plants. In fact, the pools of water left between the rocks are mini sea worlds by themselves.

Anemones in pools look like flowers, but they're really meat-eating animals.

Tiny fish dart through the water.

Starfish

Some plants and animals stick to rocks to keep from being washed away.

Muddy shores

Mudflats form where fresh water from rivers meets salty sea water. The dirt and sand they contain sticks together to make thick mud. Thousands of birds fly in from other countries to find food on mudflats.

Birds with long beaks probe in mud for slimy creatures to eat.

Looking for treasure

Besides animals, there are lots of interesting things to spot on the shore, such as fossils and shells. Even on an empty beach, you can examine towering cliffs, or watch the mesmerizing motion of the waves.

This spongy mass used to contain a sea creature's eggs.

Exploring the shore

Scientists divide the shore into several zones, which are based on how much and how often the sea covers the ground. You can identify each one by what lives there.

The tides

Twice a day, the tide comes in and goes out. When the beach is mostly covered it's high tide, and when the sea's far away, it's low tide. The tides create the zones.

Splash zone

High tide reaches here.

Low tide usually falls here.

Upper zone   Middle zone   Lower zone   *

Splash zone

This bit of the shore is furthest from the sea. The few animals and plants that live here are sprayed by the tide when it's in, but never covered.

Upper zone

The tide leaves parts of this zone exposed for days at a time. Animals that live here usually have shells to retreat into for safety until the sea covers them again.

Washed-up channelled wrack

Thrift

Most of the upper zone's inhabitants are shelled creatures called barnacles.

Rough periwinkle

Lichens are plants which grow on stones in the splash zone.

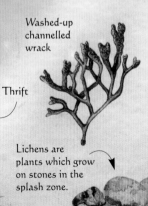

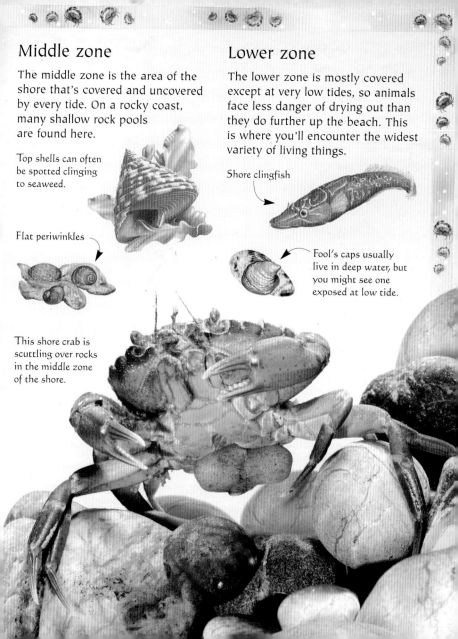

Middle zone

The middle zone is the area of the shore that's covered and uncovered by every tide. On a rocky coast, many shallow rock pools are found here.

Top shells can often be spotted clinging to seaweed.

Flat periwinkles

This shore crab is scuttling over rocks in the middle zone of the shore.

Lower zone

The lower zone is mostly covered except at very low tides, so animals face less danger of drying out than they do further up the beach. This is where you'll encounter the widest variety of living things.

Shore clingfish

Fool's caps usually live in deep water, but you might see one exposed at low tide.

Tough plants

Life is much tougher for a coastal plant than its inland relatives. Growing on the shore means having to survive against salt spray, strong winds and unsteady ground.

A constant struggle

Seashore plants tend to have special shapes or features that allow them to endure the harsh coastal climate, so look closely to spot them. For instance, some have thick, waxy leaves, which keep them from drying out in the wind.

Although plants aren't as widespread around the coast as they are inland, every area has different kinds for you to find.

The few trees that grow near the sea often twist into dramatic and permanent windswept shapes, like this one.

Yellow horned poppies gather fresh rainwater on their fuzzy leaves.

Sea holly, like its inland relative, has tough, hard leaves.

Marram grass leaves roll into narrow tubes in dry weather, trapping damp air inside.

On shingle beaches

Shingle beaches are made of stones and shells with a little sand mixed in. The shingle is constantly shifted by the tides, meaning only plants with deep roots can survive.

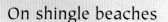

Sea bindweed

Shrubby seablite

Sea kale

*

On salt marshes

Old mudflats which are now covered in plants are called salt marshes. They're regularly engulfed by the tide, so plants that live there have to be able to deal with salt water. In fact, some have adapted so well that they can't grow without it.

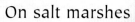

Sea lavender

*

Sea spurrey

Sea aster

On cliffs

Plants struggle hard to grow on cliffs. Most cliff plants have low, bushy shapes so their stems aren't snapped by the fierce winds. Their long roots also creep into cracks in rocks, anchoring them firmly in place.

Sea campion

Golden samphire

11

Sand dune life

Dunes are large mounds of sand which build up
when winds whirl around grasses far up the beach.
They're home to many different kinds of wildlife.

How sand dunes form

Sea lyme
grass

Sea couch
grass

Marram
grass

*

Wind

1. The wind blows
dry sand up from the
beach. It gathers in low
ridges around grasses
near the high tide line.

2. More ridges build up
around grasses beyond
the high tide line. The
growing sand pile is
called a fore dune.

3. Marram grass grows
all over the sand pile,
which keeps growing.
Its long roots stop the
dune from breaking up.

Dune plants

When the dune is big and strong, other
plants besides grasses start to grow on
it. Most of them have creeping stems,
tough leaves and small flowers. Here
are some types to look out for.

Sea rocket

Bird's foot
trefoil

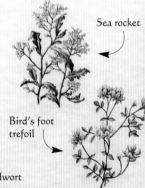

Viper's
bugloss

Sea sandwort

Animals to spot

As well as plants, sand dunes are home to lots of creepy crawlies, furry creatures and even rare toads and reptiles.

Rabbits are good for sand dunes, because their droppings help plants grow.

Foxes hunt for rabbits and may even move into their abandoned burrows.

*

Many moths and butterflies live on dunes.

Small pools of water between dunes are occasionally home to natterjack toads. Their skin gives out a nasty rubbery smell.

Dunes in danger

A growing dune is very fragile. If large gaps start to appear between the grasses, wind blows through and scatters the sand until the whole dune breaks up, leaving the animals that live there without a home. You can help preserve dunes by never digging in them or pulling out plants.

Without dunes to live on, endangered sand lizards like this would die out.

Wonderful weeds

Whether it's waving gracefully in the water, drying on the beach in the sun or slicked over rocks, you rarely have to look far on the seashore to find seaweed.

What is seaweed?

Seaweed belongs to a group of plants called algae, with no roots, leaves or flowers. It mostly grows under water, but often gets washed ashore by the sea. Some kinds stay moist on land, while others crackle up.

Bladder wrack

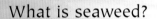

These leaf-like parts are fronds.

Thick stalk, called a stipe

This thick vein running up the middle of a frond is called a midrib.

Weed versus waves

Although it's constantly pulled about by the sea, seaweed is up to the challenge. Pods called air bladders in its fronds keep it upright in the water, and sucker-like holdfasts firmly stick it to rocks so it doesn't get swept away.

Disc-shaped

See if you can spot all the types of holdfasts shown here.

Branched

Air bladders act like swimmers' armbands, keeping the seaweed afloat.

Button-shaped

Types of seaweed

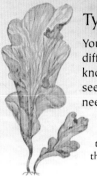

You may have noticed that seaweed comes in three different colours – green, red, and brown, like the knotted wrack below. All three kinds can be seen on most shores, although you'll need to look in different areas to find them.

Green seaweeds, like this sea lettuce, grow in the upper and middle zones.

Red seaweeds are usually small. They live in rock pools and shallow water.

A closer look

Even a quick search on a beach reveals seaweed in many shapes and sizes. You might even notice other things living on the fronds. See how many kinds you can spot, and if anything is attached.

The white marks on this saw wrack are tiny tubes with worms inside.

Tangle has many thin, flat "fingers".

Tufts of red seaweed on knotted wrack

Hornwrack appears to be seaweed, but it's not. It's clusters of very small sea creatures.

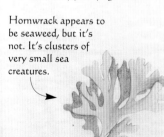

Weather forecasting

It's said that a type of seaweed called sea belt can predict the weather. If you find a piece that's limp and moist, rain is coming. But if it's crispy, the weather will be fine.

Sea belt looks like a piece of ribbon with wavy edges.

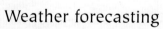

Plant or animal?

The seashore is so full of peculiar wildlife that it's sometimes hard to tell exactly what's what. All the things on these pages are animals, although they look like plants.

Anemones

Anemones live firmly attached to hard surfaces. When the tide is out they look like glistening pods, but under water they open up into vicious predators with poisonous tentacles.

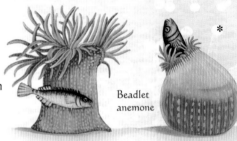

Beadlet anemone

These anemones
have attached
themselves
to a crab.

To catch their dinner, anemones wait until a small animal swims near.

The tentacles sting their prey and pull it into the anemone's gaping mouth.

Corals

Corals are made of many tiny animals called polyps. They can be entirely soft, or have hard skeletons outside their bodies. These skeletons join into groups known as colonies, which in turn form enormous coral reefs.

The gruesomely named dead man's fingers coral grows off shore. You might find it washed up on the beach after a storm.

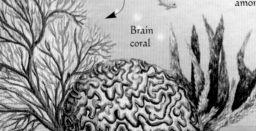

Sea fan

Little fish live among corals.

Brain coral

Elkhorn coral

16

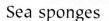

Sea sponges

Sponges grow all over the world, on the seabed or on rocks in the lower zone. Each one is actually lots of microscopic creatures inside a squishy outer "skeleton". People use the empty skeletons as natural bath sponges.

Purse sponge often grows on seaweed.

Mermaid's gloves have openings that regularly squirt out water.

Sea oranges are found in shallow water.

Waste water squirts out of the holes in these flowery shapes.

Little squirts

Sea squirts are very strange. The babies, which look like tadpoles, swim through the sea looking for a hard surface to stick to. They then grow into jelly-like adults, as shown above.

Animals in disguise

A few sea creatures have bodies that are specially adapted to fool other animals into thinking they are plants. This allows them to hide from enemies, or sneak up on prey.

This is a sea dragon. It's a type of fish, but it looks more like seaweed.

Prickles and poison

Headless creatures with poisonous spikes and the ability to clone themselves sound like something from a science fiction movie, but they actually exist on the seashore.

Living cucumbers

Despite their name, sea cucumbers are animals, not vegetables. When threatened, they spurt strings of sticky (and sometimes poisonous) guts all over an opponent. The cucumber escapes, and new guts grow back in a few weeks.

Sea cucumbers spray guts from their back ends all over an enemy.

A ball of thorns

Sea urchins are not to be messed with. Their hard, round bodies are covered with many sharp, moveable spikes, each one loaded with poison. The urchin's mouth, on the underside of its body, is filled with razor-sharp teeth.

After an urchin dies, its spikes fall off. All that's left is its skeleton, which is called a test.

An urchin moves around using suckers called tube feet that sprout from between its spikes.

Sea potatoes are a type of urchin. Their small spines look like a coat of fur.

Stars of the ocean

Starfish and their close relatives, brittle stars, have bodies made of several arms joined at the centre. If an arm is broken off, the starfish will grow a new one and, amazingly, the detached arm might also grow into a new starfish.

*

Like an urchin, a starfish has spikes on its body, although they look more like little bumps.

A cushion star's dull body and small size make it hard to spot.

A brittle star can sacrifice an arm to escape from danger – in this case, a hungry flatfish.

Deadly diners

If you spot a starfish on top of a shellfish, it might be feeding. The starfish uses powerful suckers on its arms to prise the shell open a little, then turns its stomach inside-out to reach inside and digest its victim.

This starfish is using its suckered arms to wrestle open a shell.

Scales and fins

Many types of fish live, feed and breed around the shore. Their range of body shapes and colours makes some very obvious, but others can be trickier to spot.

Finding fish

A lot of fish live far out at sea, although you'll still see quite a few if you stay around rock pools, estuaries, bays or any shallow water. Some fish live on their own, and others swim in groups called shoals.

A lumpsucker uses this sucker on its belly to anchor itself to rocks.

Sand smelts are usually seen swimming in shoals near the water's surface.

Flatfish like this dab hide in sand on the seabed. Their colour allows them to blend in.

Fish food

Despite having no teeth, many fish feed on other animals, swallowing worms or sucking molluscs right out of their shells. You might also spot them nibbling plants or poking around for tiny creatures in mud and sand.

A corkwing wrasse crushes shelled creatures between its thick lips.

Eggs to fry

Almost all fish lay eggs, which hatch into tiny babies called fry. Sometimes, one or both of the parents protects the eggs until they hatch. Look out for eggs stuck on weeds, and colourful male fish showing off to plainer females before they mate.

Hatching babies

Seahorses are odd fish, both in looks and behaviour. Males carry the female's eggs in a pouch on their bellies.

Female tompot blennies lay eggs in rocky crevices.

A rainbow wrasse starts life as a dull brown female, then changes into a bright male as it grows up.

Female wrasse

Male wrasse

Self defence

Fish are eaten by larger animals, so they need to be able to protect themselves. They usually hide in seaweeds or sand, but some can change colour to match the scenery. A few types deter foes with poison.

This scorpion fish's patterned body warns enemies, "Don't eat me, I'm poisonous!"

A worm pipefish can easily hide among thin seaweeds.

Body armour

Some creatures that live on the seashore have several legs, and hard body coverings to protect them from greedy enemies. These creatures are crustaceans.

Crusty crabs

Crabs are a common sight on most shores, scuttling sideways with their claws held high to frighten away attackers. The smallest crabs are barely bigger than a pea, but the largest, the Japanese spider crab, grows up to 3.7m (12ft) wide.

An edible crab's shell has a wavy edge that looks like pastry crust.

*

Most crabs have eight legs and two claws.

Thornback spider crabs have hairy-looking shells.

Getting undressed

Most crabs shed their shells once in a while to let their bodies expand, then grow a new one. Hermit crabs are different. They grow hard coverings on their front parts and use another animal's empty shell to protect their soft rear.

This hermit crab has just found itself a new suit of armour.

Lurking lobsters

Lobsters are shy beasts that like to lurk in secret hideaways, so the best place to look for one is a rocky crevice or hole. You can recognize them by their jointed bodies, long feelers and huge claws. Many people think lobsters are red, but in fact most are blue or green.

Lobsters have fan-shaped tails. Here, it's tucked under the body.

The large claw cracks open shells and the smaller one tears meat.

Sensitive feelers

Shrimps and prawns

Prawns and similar many-legged crustaceans swim around in shallow sea water and rock pools, waving their long feelers around to detect food.

Shrimps are almost see-through in water.

A chameleon prawn can change colour to hide itself.

Beach hoppers look a little like jumping woodlice.

Sticking around

Unlike other crustaceans, barnacles don't move. They glue their bodies to a hard surface, forming a dome with their armour. To feed, they unfurl their feathery legs through a narrow hatch in the top of the dome.

When they're under water, barnacles flick out their legs to catch prey.

Seashells

Walk along almost any beach and you'll find empty shells, the former homes of living things. If you're lucky, you might even see one complete with its slimy owner.

Animals with shells

Many animals have shells, but the type you're most likely to see on the shore are molluscs. These include snails, oysters and squid. Most molluscs – though not all – have their shells outside their bodies.

A squid's shell, called a pen, is inside its body.

This murex shell used to have an animal inside.

A pen looks like this.

*

Single shells

All the molluscs that live in the sea have either a single shell or two shells hinged together. Single-shelled sea creatures belong to the same family of animals as garden snails, and are known as gastropods.

A pelican's foot has a growth on its shell shaped like the bird's webbed toes.

Slipper limpets are often found on top of one another in chains of up to nine shells.

Double shells

Creatures called bivalves have two shells that are joined at a hinge, and which open and close like a book. Bivalves can move around surprisingly well, burrowing or, in a few cases, swimming away from danger.

In the water, scallops can swim away from enemies by clapping their two shells together.

This cockle isn't poking out its tongue. It uses this muscular foot to drag itself along the beach.

Mussels ooze out glue so they can stick to rocks.

Sea food

Molluscs come in both meat and plant-eating varieties. Gastropods use their saw-like tongues to scrape plants off rocks, or to drill holes in other animals' shells and eat their soft bodies. Many bivalves suck tiny living things called plankton out of the sea.

This meat-eating dog whelk is stretching out its sensitive feelers to detect a victim among the stones.

Blue-rayed limpets stick to the oarweed that they feed on.

In real life, these plankton are too small to see. There are countless numbers in the sea.

Birds on the beach

Muddy shores and quiet beaches are good places for birdwatching. When the tide goes out, it leaves behind hundreds of the tiny creatures that birds feed on.

Wading in

Waders are birds that spend most of their time feeding in sand or muddy water. The best place to see them is an estuary (a place where a river meets the sea). Mud can be dangerous, so don't try to get too close.

*

Black-headed gulls stomp on sand to lure worms to the surface.

Turnstones lift up pebbles to find shelled animals.

This avocet's long legs allow it to walk on wet ground without dirtying its feathers.

Sanderlings dart along the shore looking for shrimps and molluscs.

Wader watching

Most waders live in one country for part of the year, then fly to another to breed – sometimes as far away as Antarctica. April and September are the times of year when you're most likely to spot flocks of birds on their travels.

Hundreds of thousands of bar-tailed godwits visit Britain's coasts in winter.

Feeding together

Every type of bird on the shore eats different things, which means that lots of species can feed together peacefully on the same beach. A handy clue to what a bird eats is the shape of its beak.

Curlews use their slim, curved beaks to probe for tiny buried creatures.

Look for rows of little holes left behind in the sand by a dunlin's jabbing beak.

This oystercatcher has a long, strong beak for smashing mussel shells.

Nests and babies

Waders lay their eggs on beaches or grassy fields. Some build nests and others just scrape a hollow in the ground. This leaves the eggs and chicks wide open to attack, but they're hard to spot among the rocks and sand.

Little ringed plover eggs have a pattern which helps them blend into the shingle.

Clifftop birds

The rocky cliff faces that rise up along coasts
might seem like dangerous places to live, yet
they suit some types of birds perfectly.

Cliff bird features

Most cliff birds belong to one of three different
bird families: auks, gulls and terns. These types
of birds tend to be quite large, with black and
white feathers and harsh, squawking calls. They
also have webbed feet to help them swim.

Puffins are auks. They
are agile swimmers,
but awkward on land.

Herring gull

Gulls are a common
sight on almost
every shore.

Terns have forked
tails and slim,
sharp beaks.

Great black-
backed gull

Fulmars spend
hours gliding
over the sea.

Soaring seabirds

When the wind blows in from the sea and
cliffs block its path, the only way it can go
is up. Birds stretch their wings and glide on
this rising air. Gliding uses much less
energy than flapping, allowing them to stay
aloft longer and look for food further afield.

Catch of the day

Almost all birds that live on cliffs catch fish. Some hover over the water in one spot, dropping suddenly to catch the fish unawares. Others skim lightly over the water's surface, or go diving and catch their dinner beneath the waves.

Manx shearwaters almost touch, or "shear", the sea with their wing tips.

*

Razorbills can grab several fish in one go.

Storm petrels flutter over the sea at night, to avoid enemies.

Gannets dive from spectacular heights to catch fish. Look for their bright yellow heads.

*

Cliff safety

Always take care around cliffs – don't try to climb them or go near the edge, and never disturb a bird's nesting site. The safest way to look at seabirds on clifftops is from a distance, through binoculars.

Kittiwakes are small gulls with black legs. This one is on a cliff, but you might also see them on coastal buildings or piers.

Finding a partner

Like all birds, seashore birds pair up to mate and have babies. First, the birds have to impress each other with fancy displays. This is called courtship. Most couples stay together their whole lives after courtship has taken place.

Before mating, black-headed gulls run side-by-side with their heads down. *

The male gull also coughs up food as a gift for the female. *

Cliff colonies

There are few trees and bushes near the coast, so cliff birds build their nests on rocks, cliffs and islands. Some live in groups of a thousand or more, each one nesting just out of pecking distance of the others. A few birds, such as puffins, dig burrows to house their eggs.

Gannets nest in huge flocks. The same couples return to the same rocky islands to breed every year.

Shags make their nests out of twigs and seaweed.

Nestless wonders

Surprisingly, some cliff birds don't make a home for their eggs at all. Instead, they lay them directly on the rocks. Since a fall would shatter them, the eggs are specially shaped so they can't roll away.

Guillemots lay a single pear-shaped egg on a ledge. Its shape makes it roll in circles, not off the cliff edge.

Growing up

Baby cliff birds emerge from their eggs into a dangerous world of chilling winds and hungry enemies. Luckily, they have fluffy feathers to keep them warm and make them hard to see. These are replaced by smooth ones as the chick grows.

Although this herring gull chick is in plain view on the top of a cliff, its brown feathers fool enemies into thinking it's a stone.

The chick will one day have snowy white feathers and a colourful beak, like its parent.

Animal hide and seek

Beaches sometimes appear to have no life on them at all, but looks can be deceiving. Many seashore animals are very good at hiding themselves.

Buried beasts

Some sea creatures are very efficient diggers, burrowing down into the sand at top speed to avoid danger. When the tide is out, they burrow deeper to find moisture. Most of these diggers are found on the lower shore.

This masked crab is visiting the surface. It normally lives in the sand.

Watch for sand eels disappearing down into the sand near to the sea.

In the mud

Creatures that live in mud move around less than sand-dwellers, and tend to live deeper down. Their bodies have long tubes that reach to the surface for feeding and removing waste.

If you were to dig deep on a muddy beach, you might find these shells.

Peppery furrow shell

Common otter shell

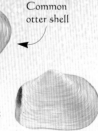

Blunt gaper

Signs in the sand

You probably won't have much luck finding buried creatures if you dig randomly in the sand or mud. The secret to finding them lies on the surface, where they leave hints to their location. You'll have to dig fast to see the animals before they burrow away.

Sea potatoes like this one leave paw-shaped imprints.

Casts are squiggly piles of sand that buried worms have squeezed out of their bodies.

It's not hard to guess what made this star-shaped mark.

Sand starfish

*

When this razor shell buries itself, it leaves a hole with water squirting out.

Wily worms

A number of worms are found on the shore, but you'll rarely see them on the surface. Like their relatives in gardens, they dig burrows in the ground or live under rocks, safe from peckish birds.

Look for ribbon worms under stones. They grow up to 50cm (20in) long.

Ribbon worm

*

A sea mouse is actually a worm that lives in the ocean. Its name refers to its furry-looking body.

Lugworm

33

Rare sightings

Some animals, such as gulls, are almost a guaranteed sight when you're on the shore. Others are much rarer or only live in certain places, but it's always worth being on the lookout.

Octopuses

Octopuses keep a low profile, making their homes in narrow, rocky crevices and only coming out at dusk and dawn to hunt. A pile of empty crab shells might be a sign of an octopus living nearby.

Common octopuses are actually much less common than the curled variety.

Look for a curled octopus like this one hiding in large rock pools.

*

Whales and dolphins

Dolphins are curious, friendly animals, so you might see them swimming alongside your boat if you go sailing. Whales are more often seen in the distance, rising up to blow water through holes in their heads.

*

Bottle-nosed dolphin

Porpoises are closely related to dolphins, but have smaller, blunt snouts.

A whale isn't a fish, it's a mammal, like you. Dolphins are mammals too.

Seals

Although seals aren't rare animals, they're hard to spot because they spend most of their time out at sea. The best time to see one is during the breeding season in June and July, when many gather on sandbanks.

Grey seals like this one live in small groups on remote, rocky shores.

Seals have short, sleek fur. A common seal's fur is always speckled.

The shark family

Despite their reputation for being huge man-eaters, sharks come in many sizes, and very few types attack people. Surfers sometimes encounter large sharks, but you're more likely to spot small ones like dogfish.

Thornback ray   *

Lesser spotted dogfish lurk near sandy seabeds, hunting for crabs.

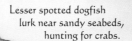

Rays are related to sharks. They swim by flapping their broad, wing-like fins.

Rock pools

Rock pools form wherever water gathers in hollows between stones and boulders on the shore. Many are teeming with life, making them a fascinating sight.

A shelter on the shore

Rock pools are very useful to many sea animals. When the tide's out, they're a refuge for creatures that need to stay wet. Deeper pools protect delicate animals that can't withstand pounding waves.

*

Low tide

High on the shore, rock pools are cut off from the sea when the tide is out. The animals are left to cope with salt, dry air and, in summer, fierce heat. Many creatures sit tight and wait for the sea to cover them again, while others hide or move.

Limpets stick firmly to the rocks.

Starfish crawl to the shelter of nearby seaweed clusters.

Blennies drag themselves from pool to pool using a pair of thin, stiff front fins.

Anemones stay moist when the tide's out by bunching up tightly into blobs.

*

High tide

A rock pool truly comes alive when the sea covers it at high tide. Fish take the chance to move to a new pool, anemones reach into the water to grab food, and slimy creatures slither over the rocks.

Breadcrumb sponges suck tiny morsels of food from the water.

Slippery butterfish squeeze between the rocks.

Seaweeds wave in the water, hiding little fish from hungry attackers.

Sea slugs crawl around looking for sponges to eat.

Things to remember

If you want to have a good look around a rock pool, it helps to be well prepared. To stay safe, always wear shoes with sturdy grips to avoid slipping on the wet rocks, and don't touch any animals – you might hurt them, or they might even hurt you. If you move a stone to look underneath, put it back afterwards. It could be an animal's home.

Rocks make great hiding places for small creatures.

Treasure hunting

Hunting for interesting animals or objects is a great way to spend a day on the shore. You might not find pirates' gold, but there are plenty of other treasures to discover.

Where to begin

A good place to start a treasure hunt is the strandline, the furthest point reached by the high tide. The sea leaves behind an intriguing hotch-potch of objects.

These glass pieces have been rubbed smooth by the waves.

Looking for life

Normally, you don't have to explore a beach for long before you find some sort of living thing. The strandline is an especially good place to spot creatures that have been brought ashore by the tide.

Beach hoppers leap around on rotting seaweed.

Portuguese men-of-war are related to corals. They can sting even when they wash up dead, so don't touch!

Look out for tiny long-clawed porcelain crabs. This one is actual size.

38

Animal signs

Even if you don't see many animals, you can search for things that they've left behind. Look closely and you could see anything from empty shells to feathers and bones.

Empty crab shells are pale on the inside.

Seabirds leave footprints in wet sand. A gull made this set.

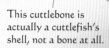

This cuttlebone is actually a cuttlefish's shell, not a bone at all.

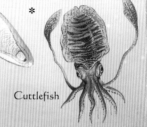

Cuttlefish

Eggs and egg cases

Many types of sea creatures, including molluscs and fish, lay eggs. Most of these eggs come in strangely shaped soft cases, which you might spot on rocks and seaweed, or washed up on the sand.

This is an empty dogfish egg case, also known as a mermaid's purse.

Flat netted dog whelk cases are left in rows on eel grass.

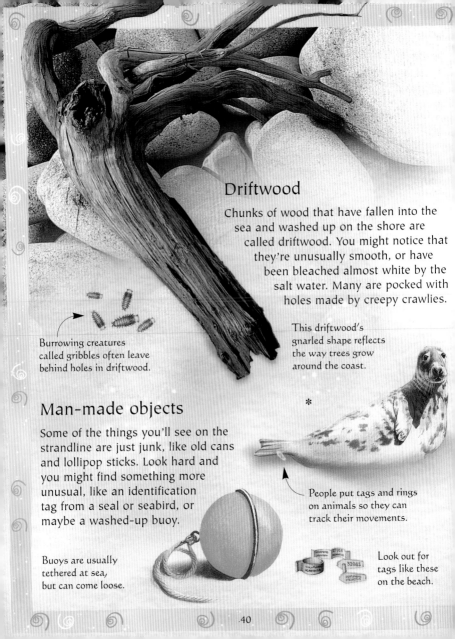

Driftwood

Chunks of wood that have fallen into the sea and washed up on the shore are called driftwood. You might notice that they're unusually smooth, or have been bleached almost white by the salt water. Many are pocked with holes made by creepy crawlies.

Burrowing creatures called gribbles often leave behind holes in driftwood.

This driftwood's gnarled shape reflects the way trees grow around the coast.

Man-made objects

Some of the things you'll see on the strandline are just junk, like old cans and lollipop sticks. Look hard and you might find something more unusual, like an identification tag from a seal or seabird, or maybe a washed-up buoy.

People put tags and rings on animals so they can track their movements.

Buoys are usually tethered at sea, but can come loose.

Look out for tags like these on the beach.

Stones and shells

Even if you don't find anything else, it's still worth checking the strandline for distinctive shells and stones. Keep an eye out especially for odd shapes and colours, or patterns and stripes.

It's OK to look under seaweed stuck to rocks, but don't pull it off.

Pebble art

Seashore pebbles are ideal for decorating, because of their smooth surface. A little imagination can turn a pebble into a crab, a bug, a face, or anything you want it to be.

You will need:
- smooth pebbles of different sizes
- assorted acrylic paints
- sheets of paper
- a pencil
- paintbrushes
- clear varnish

Keep the pebbles on the paper as you work, to avoid stains.

1. Wash the pebbles. When they're dry, paint them white and leave the paint to dry.

2. Try out some designs on paper, then paint them onto your pebbles.

These pebbles have been painted with a seaside theme.

3. Leave the pebbles on some clean paper while the paint dries. Add a coat of varnish, if you like.

Seaside rocks

The shape of a rocky coastline and its cliffs, bays and pebbles tells a tale of the way time passes and the changes it brings to the landscape.

Tiny fragments

Most rocks found at the coast, like the ones shown here, start life inland. Rivers and streams wash dirt and mud into the sea, where they settle in layers. The bits, called sediment, are then squashed down by more layers of sediment above them, and gradually change into rock.

Limestone often has bits of shells mixed in with its sediment.

Chalk is a type of limestone. It's a soft, crumbly rock.

Hard and soft

Over hundreds of millions of years, rock builds up in layer upon layer. Some parts are very hard, while others are softer. The sea wears away the soft rocks easily, creating a bay, while cliffs are made when it breaks chunks off the hard parts.

The pounding waves wore this bay out of soft rock.

Arches and stacks

When bays develop along the coast, long strips of rock are sometimes left sticking out into the sea. These are known as headlands.

As more years pass, the sea might eventually batter the headland away too, carving out caves or impressive natural stone arches.

*

Waves hammer at all sides of the headland. Pieces of rock fall off.

After many hundreds of years, the water has worn the rock through.

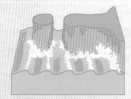

Eventually, the arch collapses and leaves behind a tower called a stack.

Pebbles on the beach

The largest lumps of rock that fall from a cliff or headland stay where they fall, but small ones get rubbed together in the sea, becoming smooth pebbles. A pebble's shape can give you a clue to the sort of rock it is.

Pebbles with coloured bands came from finely layered rocks.

*

The constant rolling of the tide sometimes creates cigar-shaped quartzite pebbles.

Many pebbles of sandstone, a sedimentary rock, are oval.

Hard granite often forms into ball-shaped pebbles.

Flat pebbles are often made of a rock called schist.

Sandy shores

Sand is what's left of rocks after millions of years of wear and tear. Pick up a handful and you could be touching something a dinosaur once walked on.

How does sand form?

Sand is a mixture of tiny particles brought to the coast by rivers, and rocks broken from cliffs. Over time, the sea pounds them into ever-smaller pieces until they become fine bits.

These are the materials that make up the sand particles on most beaches.

A crystal called quartz

A crystal called feldspar

Rocks, such as limestone and shale

Sand sculptures

If you've ever made a sandcastle, you'll know that moist sand is excellent for building. Some seaside towns even hold sand-sculpting contests to create all kinds of large and elaborate displays.

The beaches of Brazil are famous for amazing sculptures like this one. Some take days to build.

Sand ornaments

When you leave the beach, try taking home a bag of sand and using it to make a long-lasting souvenir.

You will need:
❀ 400g (14oz) sand ❀ 200g (7oz) cornflour ❀ old spoon ❀ paper ❀ 250ml (8fl oz) water ❀ old pan

This three-part sea monster is displayed on blue paper.

1. Mix the ingredients into the saucepan. Stir them thoroughly over a low heat.

2. When the mix has thickened, take it off the heat. Leave it on some paper to cool.

3. While the mix is still soft, mould it into any shape you like. Then leave it to dry.

Types of sand

Not all sand is alike. Its texture and colour varies, depending on what's in it. Volcanic rock creates gritty black sand, while pure white beaches are finely ground-up coral.

Natural glass, called obsidian, can be found on volcanic beaches.

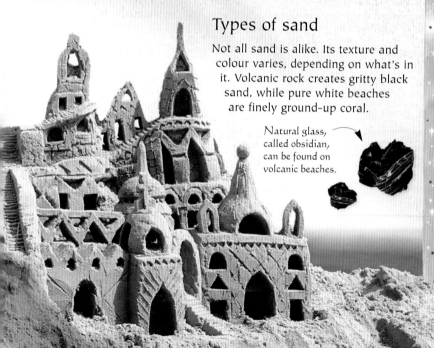

Wind and waves

The sea is never still. The wind whips it into waves and spray, while tides move it back and forth.

Sea breezes

You might have noticed it's breezy around the coast. This is because air moves from cool places to warm ones, and the sea and land are usually at different temperatures. Coastal winds can push sailboats along, and turn windmills to generate power.

Boats like this catch the wind in their sails.

Birth of a wave

When the wind blows over the ocean's surface, it creates ripples. Large ripples grow into peaks called crests, which start to travel faster and turn into waves. According to folklore, every seventh wave is more powerful than the others, but big waves are actually much less predictable

Going nowhere

If you've ever seen a gull bobbing on the water, you may have wondered how it effortlessly stays in the same spot as waves pass by. It's because waves are just changes in the shape of the ocean's surface, so although they travel forwards, the water itself does not.

A surfer selects a single wave and rides it all the way to the shore.

Breaking waves

When a wave reaches the shore, its crest collapses and the wave is said to have broken. The shape of a breaking wave depends on how steeply the shore slopes into the water, so see if you can spot the difference.

The foam on top of a wave is called a whitecap.

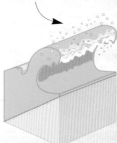

*

In shallow water, the bottom of the wave drags on the ground. The top moves faster and breaks first.

Spilling breakers happen on gently sloping coasts. The waves break slowly, so the crest spills gently.

A plunging breaker occurs on steep shores. The waves curl completely over at the top and crash noisily down.

Building a beach

Waves are responsible for creating beaches. As they break on the shore and surge forwards, they leave behind lots of sediment. If enough remains when the water creeps back, a beach eventually builds up. The sea can carry sediment all along the coast when waves break at an angle to the shore.

Barriers called groynes are built to keep the moving sea from washing the sand away.

Fossil hunting

Beaches can be good places to go on a fossil hunt. Finding fossils gives you a fascinating glimpse of creatures that lived in the prehistoric world.

What is a fossil?

Fossils are the remains of ancient living things. They're usually made of an animal's hard parts, such as its teeth, bones or shell, but they can also be imprints of things left behind in mud.

Fossilized shark tooth

Millions of years ago, this stone was soft mud with a plant stuck in it.

Forming a fossil

These pictures show how a sea creature called an ammonite becomes fossilized.

*

1. The ammonite dies and sinks. Its body rots, leaving the shell.

2. Time passes. Layers of sand build up, burying the shell deeper.

3. As centuries pass, the shell is broken down and replaced by rock.

4. Eventually, a shell-shaped rock is left behind. This is a fossil.

Seaside fossils

Most life from the past vanished without a trace, because plants and animals' soft bodies decayed over time. Sea creatures with hard shells, though, were perfect for fossilization. Some are ancestors of animals that roam the seas today.

Belemnites look like stone bullets, but they're the fossilized skeletons of squid-like creatures.

Trilobites lived over 245 million years ago, before dinosaurs existed.

*

*
Trilobite fossil in stone

Here's how a living belemnite might have looked.

Where to look

Not all shores are suitable for fossil hunting, although some are better than others. A beach surrounded by chalky cliffs is often a good place to start. There's more about where to look for fossils on the Usborne Quicklinks Website at www.usborne-quicklinks.com.

Limestone often contains fossilized shells, or imprints of their shapes.

You might find snail shell fossils embedded in rock, or – if you're lucky – on their own.

This is a fossilized sea urchin's skeleton. The holes show where rows of spikes would have been.

A world of seashells

Shells vary in size, shape and shade from place to place.
Looking for them is enjoyable wherever in the world
you are, but be sure only to pick up empty ones.

Family matters

Shells that belong to the same families
generally live in similar conditions,
even if they're in different
parts of the world.

Wentletraps live
in shallow water
on any sandy shore.

Precious wentletrap

Crenulated
wentletrap

Cool water shells

The cool seas surrounding
northern Europe and North
America are mostly home
to small, tough shells.

European
screw shells

Hallia

Mediterranean shells

The waters of the Mediterranean
Sea between Europe and Africa are
warm and calm. Many of its shells
are small, or thin and delicate.

Rustic dove
shell

Date mussel

Rosy
tooth shell

Tropical shells

Tropical seas, around Australia, Africa and the Caribbean, contain the widest variety of large or colourful shells.

White banded bubble shells

Distaff spindle

King helmet

Conch shells like this are found in the Bahamas. It's said you can hear the sea if you hold one to your ear.

Collecting and cleaning

Most of the fun of shell collecting is hunting for them, but you might want to take a few home too. Clean them thoroughly with warm, soapy water and a soft paintbrush, then leave them to dry on some paper.

Most empty bivalve shells are missing one half, though you might find a few with both.

It's wise not to buy exotic shells like these from shops. The animals they came from were probably killed illegally.

Seaside signals

Although the seashore is enjoyable to visit, it has many hazards too. Both the people on the shore and sailors at sea need signs to help keep them out of danger.

Safety on the shore

When the tide comes in, the water level can rise surprisingly fast. Flags or signs on the beach give warnings about whether conditions are safe.

Yellow and red flags mark out an area where lifeguards are on patrol.

A red flag means it's not safe to enter the sea.

Not all dangers carry warning signs. Help keep yourself safe by not going off exploring alone, and staying away from caves when the tide's coming in.

Lifebuoys like this can be thrown to swimmers in trouble.

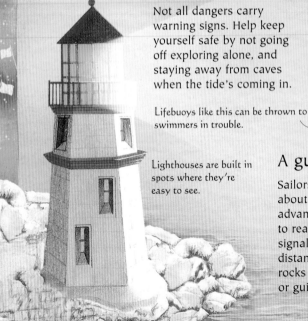

Lighthouses are built in spots where they're easy to see.

A guiding light

Sailors may need to know about a hazard far in advance, so they have time to react. Lighthouses flash signals to boats over long distances, warning them of rocks hidden under the water or guiding them through fog.

Message buoys

Buoys are floating plastic balls or platforms which give information. They can be used for anything from marking a safe route through the waters to monitoring weather, mooring boats or sending emergency signals.

A buoy with these markings warns that the area is dangerous.

This buoy is supposed to mark a path for ships, but these sea lions are using it as a place to have a nap.

This pattern on a buoy is used to indicate a safe area.

Flying the flag

Ships don't fly flags from their masts for decoration. Each one stands for both a letter of the alphabet and a message, which can be recognized by other sailors.

"A"   *   "N"   "C"

This flag is the letter "A". It's displayed when a diver's swimming under the boat.

"N" means "No" and "C" means "Yes". Flying them together is a distress signal.

Ocean bounty

Fish and other seafoods are well-known ocean resources. But the sea has many other treasures to offer, including fuels, medicines and gems.

Jewels of the ocean

The most precious jewels that come from the sea are pearls, which form inside a very small number of oysters. Other shells are used to make jewellery too, such as the shiny mother-of-pearl coating inside top shells and abalones.

Mother-of-pearl shimmers blue or grey in the light.

This oyster might be the only one in 10,000 that contains a pearl.

Feeding on weed

Seaweed is very versatile. It's a common ingredient in many oriental foods and, believe it or not, seaweed extract is also used to thicken ice cream and is even found in common household items such as toothpaste.

Dulse is an edible seaweed.

Useful waste

Seabird droppings, also known as guano, are one of the most effective forms of natural fertilizer – 30 times richer than farmyard manure. Guano is gathered from sea cliffs and exported around the world.

Layers of cormorant guano can be many metres thick.

Lifesavers

The healing power of plants has been recognized for many centuries, but the next generation of medicines might come from the ocean. These could include painkillers, surgical glue, cancer-fighting drugs and much more.

Some corals are so similar to human bone, they're used in operations.

Scientists think they might be able to make painkillers from deadly poison found in cone shells.

Certain types of sea slugs are being tested as a source of drugs to treat memory loss.

Fossil fuel

Over a fifth of the world's oil comes from the sea bed. Oil formed millions of years ago when the remains of sea creatures and plants sank to the bottom of the sea and broke down into an oozing black liquid, beneath layers of sand and rock.

When prehistoric sea animals and plants like these died, their bodies very slowly turned into oil.

Save Our Seas

For many centuries, people existed in harmony with the sea. In recent times, our changing lifestyles have started to make human beings an enemy to ocean life.

Oil spills

Lots of oil that people burn for fuel is transported in huge ships called tankers. If oil accidentally spills into the ocean, it forms a pool called a slick on the water's surface. Washed-up slicks pollute beaches and can kill wildlife.

*

Seabirds can't keep warm if their feathers are oily, so they die. Conservationists help the birds by scrubbing them clean.

Overfishing

Today's enormous fishing nets and use of electronic equipment to find fish lead to bigger catches than ever before. If fishermen catch too many of one type of fish, they risk causing it to die out. This is called overfishing.

Fishing with large nets can lead to other animals being caught along with the fish.

Many people are campaigning for fishing nets with larger holes, which allow young fish to escape and breed.

In 1977, fishing for herring was banned in the North Sea so their numbers could increase.

Beach invaders

Millions of holidaymakers visit beaches every year, with hotels constantly being built to accommodate them. The more of the coast that people take over, the less room there is for animals.

Beach tourism has driven Mediterranean monk seals to the verge of extinction.

This sea turtle comes ashore to breed. But humans on beaches scare turtles away.

What you can do

You might not be able to stop an oil slick, but you can help keep the shore clean by never leaving litter behind. At home, you could avoid eating species that are known to be overfished, or join an ocean conservation group. You can find out more on the Usborne Quicklinks Website at www.usborne-quicklinks.com.

Abandoned can-holders strangle animals. Help avoid this by cutting them up before you put them in the bin.

Myths and legends

The oceans have inspired storytellers throughout history, leading to dramatic tales of monsters, gods and ghosts. Could any of these legends be true?

King of the ocean

Many Ancient Greek myths feature gods and monsters of the deep. The ruler of them all was a god named Poseidon (known to the Romans as Neptune). He lived in an underwater palace made of coral and gems, and his anger was said to stir up violent storms.

Poseidon carried a magic trident that could create earthquakes.

Birth of a goddess

Venus, the Roman goddess of love and beauty, was born from ocean foam. She is traditionally shown standing on a giant clam shell with nature spirits called nymphs surrounding her. In Greek myths, Venus is called Aphrodite.

This picture shows the goddess Venus being born from the waves.

Animal gods

Supernatural sea dwellers are not only a feature of Greek myths. In Fiji, legend has it that the fierce shark god Dakuwanga ate fishermen, but was forced to change his ways by an octopus god who defeated him in battle.

The Fijian god Dakuwanga was said to take the form of a monstrous basking shark.

Mermaids

Mermaids were fabled creatures with a woman's top half and a fish's tail. Stories exist all over the world of sailors who saw and fell in love with these seductive sea maidens.

Moo maids

It's possible that sailors who thought they saw mermaids were actually seeing animals called sea cows. From a distance, they might look a little like humans with fish tails.

In stories, mermaids normally have long, flowing hair, which they spend hours combing.

Sand dollars are a type of urchin. Their empty shells are known as mermaids' money.

*

Up close, it's hard to imagine how anyone could mistake a sea cow for a mermaid.

Ghost ships

In the 17th and 18th centuries, reported sightings of ghostly ships were quite common. A ship called *The Flying Dutchman* was cursed to sail the world until the end of time, and even today it's rumoured to bring terrible bad luck to anyone who sees it.

German submariners claimed to see *The Flying Dutchman* during World War II.

A phantom ship called the *Libera Nos* is said to roam the oceans with a crew of skeletons.

Sea serpents

Throughout history, sailors have told tales of huge serpents swimming past their ships. Ocean-dwelling snakes really do exist but they're not very big, so the stories seem to be just that.

Most sea snakes are less than 1m (3ft) long.

Giant sea serpents like this almost certainly don't exist outside people's imaginations.

A land under the sea

The island of Atlantis was said to have been destroyed by an earthquake around 10,000BC, sinking into the sea without a trace. No one knows if it really existed or where it is, but guesses have included sites near Cuba, Gibraltar and even Antarctica.

Many stories mention the great wealth of Atlantis. Perhaps its treasures still lie beneath the waves.

Monsters of the deep

Stories of sea monsters are closely related to those of sea snakes. Perhaps the most horrifying of them all is the kraken which, according to legend, would wrap its immense tentacles around a ship to capsize it, then devour the crew.

Lake monsters, such as the mysterious Loch Ness Monster of Scotland, could be the last relatives of sea monsters – if they are real.

Real monsters?

Some of the people who claimed to see kraken and other vast sea creatures might have been describing giant squid. These creatures are known to live in the deep ocean, yet a live one has never been caught. An even larger "real monster", the colossal squid, is thought to live near the Antarctic.

No one has ever photographed a colossal squid. This computer image shows how experts think it might look.

Did you know?

Extreme eggs
The ocean sunfish lays up to 300 million eggs in one batch.

Largest fish
The largest recorded whale shark was 18m (59ft) long, and was estimated to weigh a whopping 48 tons.

Whale shark and diver

Ink-credible
Cuttlefish and squid squirt out a cloud of liquid called sepia to confuse their enemies. For many centuries, people used this to make ink.

Sepia is brown, like a cuttlefish's body.

Largest jellyfish
The largest jellyfish recorded had a body 2.29m (7.5ft) wide, with tentacles measuring 3.65m (12ft).

*

Heaviest clam
A giant clam collected from the coast of Australia weighed 262.9kg (over a quarter of a ton).

Bated breath
Sperm whales can hold their breath for up to two hours, the longest of any mammal.

Giant clam

Small fry
The world's smallest sea fish is the dwarf goby. The body of an adult fish is about 8mm (0.3in) long.

Wonder whiskers
Walrus whiskers are so stiff, Inuit people use them as toothpicks.

Walrus

Pea crab in mussel shell

*

Tiniest crabs
Pea crabs are barely 6.5mm (a quarter of an inch) long. They live and feed inside oyster and mussel shells.

Electric fish
The black torpedo ray can create electricity in its body – enough to power a TV in a short burst.

Awesome waves

The highest natural wave ever recorded was seen in the Pacific in 1933. It measured 34m (111.5ft), the height of a ten-storey building.

Tremendous tides

The greatest tidal range in the world occurs in the Bay of Fundy in Canada. The water level can rise by as much as 15m (50ft) during each tide.

Deepest ocean bed

The deepest part of the Pacific Ocean is 11.033km (6.85 miles) deep. A 1kg steel ball would take just over an hour to sink to the bottom.

Tallest mountain

Earth's tallest mountain is Mauna Kea, which rises up 10,203m (33,474ft) from the floor of the Pacific Ocean.

Highest sea cliffs

The sea cliffs around Molokai, Hawaii, are as tall as three Eiffel Towers – that's over 960m (3,150ft).

Sunken gold

Sea water contains traces of many metals, including gold. If it could be extracted, there would be enough for everyone on Earth to have their own 4g (0.14oz) piece.

Sea salt

There's enough salt in the oceans to cover the land with a layer 150m (492ft) thick.

Sea life

An estimated 80% of all living things on Earth exist beneath the ocean's surface.

Coral reefs cover only 0.7% of the ocean floor, yet contain 25% of ocean life.

INDEX

ACKNOWLEDGEMENTS

Managing designer: Karen Tomlins
Cover design: Karen Tomlins
Artwork co-ordinator: Louise Breen
Website advisor: Lisa Watts
Additional thanks to Steve Wills of the Royal National Lifeboat Institution

PHOTO CREDITS (t = top, m = middle, b = bottom, l = left, r = right)
1 Getty Images/Peter Dawson; 2&3 2004 Digital Vision; 5b 2004 Digital Vision;
6 Getty Images/Firecrest Pictures; 9b Jane Burton/Warren Photographic;
10b Ashley Cooper/Alamy; 13m Geoff Simpson/Alamy; 17b Jeffrey Jeffords/Divegallery.com;
19b FRED WINNER/JACANA/SCIENCE PHOTO LIBRARY; 21b Image100/Alamy;
22b Hal Beral/CORBIS; 27t Neil Hardwick/Alamy; 29b Image100/Alamy;
31r Celia Mannings/Alamy; 32m Jim Greenfield/imagequestmarine.com;
35t Chris Gomersall/Alamy; 39b Niall Benvie/Naturepl; 42 Lester Lefkowitz/CORBIS;
44b & 45b Getty Images/Eduardo Garcia; 46b StockShot/Alamy; 51m Botanica/OSF;
53 Steve Bly/Alamy; 54b K-PHOTOS/Alamy; 57m 2004 Digital Vision;
63b 2004 Digital Vision

ADDITIONAL ILLUSTRATORS David Ashby, Graham Austin, Bob Bampton, David Baxter, Andrew Beckett, Joyce Bee, Isabelle Bowring, Wendy Bramall, Paul Brooks, Mark Burgess, Hilary Burn, Liz Butler, Frankie Coventry, Patrick Cox, Kevin Dean, Sarah De Ath, Michelle Emblem, Denise Finney, Sarah Fox-Davies, Nigel Frey, Sheila Galbraith, Will Giles, Victoria Gooman, Victoria Gordon, Nick Harris, David Hurrell, Ian Jackson, Roger Kent, Colin King, Deborah King, Mick Loates, Alan Marks, Andy Martin, Rodney Matthews, Uwe Mayer, Rob McCaig, Dee McLean, Dee Morgan, David Nash, Gillian Platt, Cynthia Pow, David Quinn, Charles Raymond, Maggie Silver, Gwen Simpson, Ralph Stobart, George Thompson, Joan Thompson, Joyce Tuhill, Sally Volke, Phil Weare, James Woods